novum premium

Jean Dickinson

THE ADVENTURES OF A MYTHICAL COW AND HORSE

For Dreamers ages 5 to 105

novum premium

© 2018 novum publishing

ISBN 978-1-64268-026-3
Editing: novum publishing
Cover: Cheri Dickinson
Cover design, layout & typesetting: novum publishing

www.novumpublishing.com

All rights of distribution, including via film, radio, and television, photomechanical reproduction, audio storage media, electronic data storage media, and the reprinting of portions of text, are reserved.

TABLE OF CONTENTS

Introduction 7

LOCAL 9
The Cow and The Horse 11
The Cow and The Horse Get Ice Cream 13
The Cow and The Horse Get Seat Belts 15
The Cow and The Horse Go to the Library 16
The Cow and The Horse Go Skating 18
The Cow and The Horse Go Skiing 20
The Cow and The Horse Go Camping 21
The Cow and The Horse Make a Decision 24
The Cow and The Horse Go to the Circus 26
The Cow and The Horse Go to the Fair 28
The Cow and The Horse and the Ground Hog 30
The Cow and The Horse in Mud Season 32
The Cow and The Horse and the Birthday Plate 34
The Cow, The Horse and the Telephone 36
The Cow and The Horse, Thanksgiving 37
The Cow and The Horse, Helping Santa 39

UNITED STATES 41
The Cow and The Horse Go to New York 43
The Cow and The Horse Go to Florida 46
The Cow and The Horse Go West 48
The Cow and The Horse Go to Chinatown 51
The Cow and The Horse Travel to Minnesota 53
The Cow and The Horse and Sheboygan 56

FOREIGN TRAVEL 59
The Cow and The Horse Go to Norway 61
The Cow and The Horse Go to Norway Again 64
The Cow and The Horse Go to Scotland 66
The Cow and The Horse Visit England 68
The Cow and The Horse Go to Paris 70
The Cow and The Horse Go to Bordeaux 72
The Horse and the Cow Visit Bordeaux II 74
The Cow and The Horse Travel the Midi Canal 76
The Cow and The Horse Go to Hong Kong 78
The Cow and The Horse Go to Singapore 80
The Cow and The Horse Go to Thailand 82
The Cow and The Horse Go to Bali 84
The Cow and The Horse Go to Siberia 86
The Cow and The Horse Go Back to Siberia 88

INTRODUCTION

The following encounter that I had with The Cow and The Horse was the reason for this book. I hope you have as much fun reading it as I did writing it, and then, with The Cow and The Horse, revisiting some of my own most fascinating destinations.

And THANK YOU to all who listened to each poem as it appeared and then encouraged The Horse and The Cow to travel some more.
  And so I began:

The Cow sat on the running board, The Horse sat on the hood.
  OR, The Horse sat on the running board, The Cow sat on
                                            the hood.

Make up your mind, dear Jean, The Cow then said.
  If you don't, this story will never be read!

Oh, leave her alone, The Horse replied. We can change places,
                                              you know.
  I'd rather be on the running board; it's closer to the snow.

There is no snow. It's summertime, The Cow said in disgust.
  That may be true, but when winter comes it will snow, I trust.

But I'll be back in the barn by then and the snow won't bother me.

Said The Cow to The Horse, as she sat on the hood,
  Or was it The Horse who sat on the hood? Please tell me,
                                              if you would?

Happy Reading!
Jean Senstad Dickinson

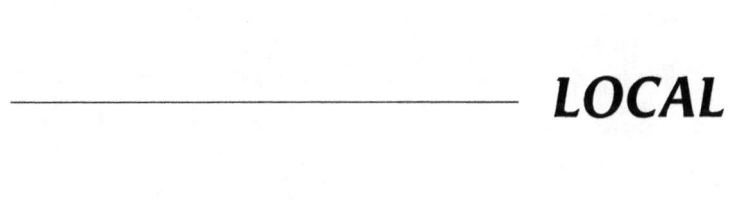

THE COW AND THE HORSE

The Cow came first from the pasture above.
   There is a car, but it doesn't move.

I'll explore just a bit—I can climb on the hood—
   I think this car will sit here for good.

Just then The Horse galloped by and saw The Cow sitting there.
   I wonder what she's doing—but I must not stare.

So The Horse stopped short and said, Hi there, Cow.
   What are you doing on that hood just now?

I think this car's stuck right here on the hill.
   They are saving it from going to yonder landfill.

You are probably right, said The Horse to The Cow.
   I'll rest on the running board. I'm tired now.

So what is your name? said The Cow to The Horse.
   It's just The Horse, capital letters, of course.

And what is your name? said The Horse to The Cow.
   My name is The Cow—Look, I'll take a bow!

Oops! Here I go—right off this hood.
   She slid to the ground and there she stood.

Are you hurt? asked The Horse, as he watched The Cow land.
   Oh no, said The Cow, but give me a hand.

Or what do you have on the end of your leg?
   Mine is a hoof. What is yours, I beg?

Mine, too, is a hoof—it isn't a hand.
   But I'll stomp my hooves right here on the land.

Is that what you want? Or would a loud 'Neigh' be best
   To acknowledge your bow? What's your request?

And so The Horse and The Cow each gained a new friend.
   If they tell their adventures, their tales won't end.

THE COW AND THE HORSE GET ICE CREAM

The Cow sat on the running board, The Horse sat on the hood,
   The Cow spoke up, Let's go someplace. I'm really in the mood.

OK, I'll drive. You can find the way.
   We'll close our eyes and concentrate since this is where we'll stay.

That's right, The Cow chimed in, We can take any course!
   Wow! We can do that! We have a car! happily cried The Horse.

We can go anywhere and be back before night.
   Good, I'm afraid of the dark, said The Cow. That will be just right.

Let's get some ice cream. I'm already exhausted from thinking,
   Said The Cow as her eyes started blinking.

So off to the ice cream store they drove in their mind.
   I'll take chocolate. I like that kind,

Said The Horse. And I'll take plain white,
   Said The Cow, If I might.

How do you eat an ice cream cone? The Cow asked in dismay.
   I don't know how to hold it—I've only eaten hay.

You take your two front hoofs to hold the cone.
   But it just slipped and fell—I should have known,

Wept The Cow. It's on the ground to stay.
   Don't cry. That's how we eat each day!

We'll eat our cones and lick our lips and then head back right now.
   Just close your eyes and we're back home, The Horse said to
                                                   The Cow.

And so they got back before dark, just as they knew they would,
   The Cow sitting on the running board, and The Horse there
                                                   on the hood.

THE COW AND THE HORSE GET SEAT BELTS

The Cow sat on the running board, The Horse sat on the hood.
   We have no seat belts, said The Cow. You know we should.

There's rope in the barn, The Horse said with delight.
   We'll figure it out and tie them up tight.

How will it work? asked The Cow. How will it attach?
   The Horse smiled, The belts could be different, they don't have
                                                         to match.

The rope for the hood could go through the car,
   Right through the door window—that's not too far.

The running board seat belt—through the windows from front
                                                               door to back.
   I'll tie the rope well and not leave any slack.

The Horse added, Now we'll be safe and drive right along
   Singing out loudly a 'safe-traveling' song.

There, now we are ready. Where shall we go?
   Perhaps to the mountains to visit some snow?

The Cow pleaded, No, that's too cold.
   Let's go south to the beach. It's warm there I'm told.

So The Cow and The Horse started their ride
   On the running board and hood—their seat belts well tied.

First they went to the South where it was hot,
   And then came back home each seat belt tied in a knot.

THE COW AND THE HORSE
GO TO THE LIBRARY

The Cow sat on the running board, The Horse sat on the Hood
   Have you heard of a Library? Maybe we can go there.
                                      Do you think we could?

The Cow hopefully asked the Horse.
   The Horse replied, Of course, of course!

Now tie your seat belt and be sure it's tight.
   The Cow exclaimed, I think it has books! I'm sure that's right!

I've heard of that, but we've never been there.
   It's right in town, but I'm not sure just where,

Said The Horse to the Cow as they traveled along
   Right into town. They just couldn't be wrong.

There it is! It must have books! screamed The Cow with delight.
   We can look at the books. There should be plenty of light

For us to enjoy and our brains to employ. Wow, that's a good word.
   Do our brains employ? Or is that just absurd?

Said The Cow to The Horse as they climbed up the stairs
   And opened the door and exclaimed, I wonder who cares

For all of these books?! It's too much for me!
   But let's look at the shelves. There is so much to see!

Here's a book about horses and children's books too!
   And all kinds of books on 'What to do!'

This is a wonderful place, I don't want to go!
   But the traffic gets heavy and we'll have to go slow.

Said The Horse to The Cow as back home they went.
   And The Cow added happily, It's been a day well spent!

THE COW AND THE HORSE GO SKATING

The Cow sat on the running board, The Horse sat on the hood.
   Let's go skating. I could try. I think we should,

Said The Cow to The Horse.
   Yes, let's try. Of course, of course.

I've watched the kids on the pond over there.
   Should there be skates for us to wear?

They wear sharp blades on a kind of shoe.
   I wonder if that is what we should do?

We have smooth hoofs on the bottom of our feet.
   Maybe we don't need skates, our smooth hoofs might work.
   That would be neat,

Said The Horse as they approached the pond.
   Please sing The Blue Danube Waltz of which I'm so fond,

Said The Cow as she stepped out on the ice and took an
                                          undignified spill.
   The Cow cried through her tears, I'll learn to skate, I will, I will!

I'll help you up. We'll get our feet working together,
   And then we'll glide along as light as a feather,

Said The Horse as they tried once more
   To glide to the music. We know the score,

Said The Cow as she moved to the music going round in
                                                       her head.
   This is just perfect. But we'll be ready for bed

When the sun goes down and we must go home
   To sleep and to dream until the next time we roam.

And so The Cow and The Horse enjoyed skating that day.
   The Cow said to the Horse, We can do this again without
                                                       going away.

THE COW AND THE HORSE GO SKIING

The Cow sat on the running board, The Horse sat on the hood.
   Let's go skiing. Do you think we could?

Said The Cow to The Horse, There's a lot of snow
   And maybe we could go slow

Down the hill that is right up there
   With a house falling down and boards to spare.

I think we could find boards that would make good skis.
   And if we can't stand up, we can go down on our knees.

Replied The Horse with enthusiasm to spare.
   So they got down from the car and headed up there

To the house falling down. They found four boards for skis.
   But this doesn't work, even on my knees!

Cried The Cow as she fell into the snow.
   Maybe a door would make a large sled. Maybe, I don't
                                      really know.

There is a door that is easy to get.
   Said The Horse, That's the best idea yet!

They both sat on the door and sped down the hill.
   This is great! We've had our first winter thrill!

It's time to go home—I guess to the Barn.
   It is winter. We better spend time where it's warm.

Said The Cow as they scampered off to the cozy warm Barn
   And could tell all their friends their exciting new Yarn.

THE COW AND THE HORSE GO CAMPING

The sun is so bright, and the weather so warm, said The Cow
                     on the running board to The Horse on the hood.
   Why don't we go camping—that would be good.

Why not! said The Horse. We must pack up our gear
   And bring lots of food since no store will be near.

We can buy groceries and things that we need
   And then we can get there going full speed.

Where will we go? Down by a lake?
   I hope that we will. Don't forget the towels we must take!

Said The Cow to The Horse as she made a long list
   Of things to remember so her mind wouldn't drift.

They packed up the car and tied seat belts tight
   And took off for a park to be there before night.

I'll set up the tent, said The Horse to The Cow.
   Can you gather wood and start the fire? Do you know how?

Oh, yes, I can. I brought a match. She took a low bow.
   Don't worry about me, said The confident Cow.

I'll get the marshmallows and hot dogs and start the fire.
   Or should we go swimming, if that's your desire,

Said The Cow to The Horse as he put up the tent.
   Yes, let's go swimming. And so off they went

To the lake in a mad dash
  And laughed as they ran in and made a great splash.

This is so much fun, but we better eat.
  The fire will dry us. This camping is neat!

So back to the fire to roast those hot dogs.
  I'm so glad the beach was sandy without any bogs.

Spread out the blanket, we can picnic nearby,
  And when it gets dark, we can see the stars in the sky.

Oh, that would be great.
  We never get to stay up very late.

Said The Cow to The Horse.
  And we can make s'mores! Of course, of course!

The stars are out. I see the Milky Way!
  This sky is more fun than the sun shining all day.

Said the Horse to The Cow.
  But I'm sleepy just now.

It's time to crawl into the tent with a blanket to keep warm
  And the tent to protect us and keep us from harm.

Good night, said The Horse as he started to snore,
  And The Cow went to sleep dreaming of camping some more,

Until the sun woke them up. It was morning, of course.
　Let's go for a swim before we eat, said The Horse.

After the swim and breakfast to eat,
　We better head back, but camping's a treat.

So tie up your belt and hang on tight.
　We'll make a sharp turn, off to the right.

We're heading back home, but we'll go the long way
　To make this adventure an exceptional day!

THE COW AND THE HORSE MAKE A DECISION

The Horse sat on the running board. The Cow sat on the hood.
  I can see farther from here. I didn't know I could.

Said The Cow. Where would you like to go?
  Hmmm. I really don't know.

Said The Horse. I'll put on my thinking cap.
  Or else we could certainly look at a map.

But do we have a map? The Cow then queried.
  No we don't, but I'm not worried.

Said The Horse. We can close our eyes. We might have
                                        something in mind.
  See what you think. Just what kind

Of place would you like? A city or ocean
  Or park, lake or town? Have you a notion

Of a place or special destination?
  We could stay here or go to a different nation.

Said The Horse. Hmmm, I'm not sure yet.
  Would we want snow, warm or a place to get wet?

The Cow shouted with glee, Let's go to a Circus! That would
                                                    be fun.
  Good idea! agreed The Horse, Let's see where we can find
                                                        one.

There is Circus Smirkus here in Vermont.
   But that's not the kind of Circus I want.

Said The Cow. I want one with lions and tigers and a great
                                                              big tent,
   Just like the one where our grandparents went.

But let's not look now, let's wait until tomorrow
   When someone we know may have a map we can borrow.

Yes, let's wait until tomorrow, said The Horse.
   And The Cow chimed in, Tomorrow, of course.

THE COW AND THE HORSE GO
TO THE CIRCUS

The Cow sat on the running board, The Horse sat on the hood.
   We made the decision to go to a circus. Today is the day
                                                          we should.

I heard there is one close by! The Cow said hopefully.
   Of course, said the Horse. We'll leave immediately.

I have sandwiches packed and my seat belt tied.
   Wow! We're up in the air! The Cow then cried.

I see a tent, a great big tent!
   Said The Horse as over the edge of the car he bent.

To see better the tent and animals below.
   I'm sure it's the Circus—We mustn't go slow

To land and get out and look at what's there.
   Do you think at a Circus they'll care if we stare?

Oh no! said The Cow. We should look all around
   And see the lions and tigers and elephants they've found.

Let's go into the tent and see what is there.
   There are people on swings and tightropes way up in the air!

That makes me wonder—how do they dare
   To swing up there and catch others? The pair

Seems to work together to do that great feat.
   I'd be scared to death, in case we'd not meet

Up in the air, way up from the ground!
  Let's just go back outside and look around.

Said The Cow to The Horse. Animals, too, performed in the tent.
  They were amazing. I'm glad we went.

But let's find a Clown. I hear they are fun, and then let's go home.
  The Clown made them laugh. They were glad they had come.

So, they got back on the car and with their seat belts tied tight,
  They headed back home and got back before night.

THE COW AND THE HORSE GO TO THE FAIR

The Cow sat on the running board, The Horse sat on the hood.
  I'd like to just roam about today, if we could.

Said The Cow. Of course, said the Horse. Let's do that and
                                    see what's just over there.
  Oh look at the buildings and flags! I think it's a Fair!

There's a building for horses with green grass outside.
  And another with cows, but they are all inside.

The Cow chimed in, I'd like to see the handmade things—
  Like rugs and clothes and furniture, even jewelry with rings.

And the building with food all baked and delicious.
  One thing about those—so beautiful, but are they nutritious?

No bakery is baking and bringing it here.
  It's all made at home. Look at the blue ribbons to cheer!

The Horse got excited. I think there's a race!
  With horses and sulkies setting the pace—

Around and around the racetrack they go—
  Don't you think this is a glorious show?

Said The Horse as he whinnied with glee—
　But sometimes I wish the winner was me.

Sadly, The Horse and The Cow turned around.
　The Horse beckoned The Cow, It's time for us to be homeward bound.

Back to the Car, their chariot with wings—
　As long as they dream up the adventures it brings.

THE COW AND THE HORSE AND THE GROUND HOG

The Cow sat on the running board, The Horse sat on the hood.
   What is that little head sticking up in the snow—over by
                                              the wood?

Asked The Cow of The Horse, Have you seen one before?
   It is some small animal. There are animals galore.

Who, or what are you? The Horse called to the little head.
   I've been sleeping so long. Should I come out of my home,
                                            or go back to bed?

I'm a Ground Hog and this is my day.
   To decide if it's going to stay Winter or turn to Spring.
                                    Silly people believe what I say.

What are you two doing there sitting on a car?
   We go on many adventures. They could be near or far.

The Cow said with a smile.
   Would you like to come along for a ride, for maybe just a mile?

I'd love to go with you, but not very far.
   I'll share my seat belt so you'll be safe on our car.

Said The Horse. We'll just go into town.
   After that you can decide to stay out, or go in and lie down.

So the Ground Hog came out and climbed up on the car.
   The Horse moved over, tied the seat belt tight so they would
                                              stay where they are

And not fall off and land on the ground.
   The three friends took off and had a good look around.

Thanks heaps for the ride. That was great fun! said the happy
                                            Ground Hog,
   I'll tell all my friends and Mr. Big Green Frog.

The Horse called to the Ground Hog, Did you see your shadow,
                                                        or not?
   Oh, my! said the Ground Hog as he dove into his hole, I guess
                                                        I forgot.

THE COW AND THE HORSE IN MUD SEASON

The Cow sat on the running board, The Horse sat on the hood.
   It has stopped raining. Maybe we can take a ride. I think
                                              we could.

Said The Cow to The Horse
   And The Horse replied, Good idea. Of course, of course.

I like to go before the leaves come out.
   Then we can see to the top of the hills and all about.

The trees look like silhouettes and charcoal sketches
   And there's grass showing with snow still in patches.

The hardtop roads are fun to go on.
   But let's try the dirt roads just for fun.

This road is bumpy with many ruts.
   Hang on tight! It's challenging driving—no ifs, ands, or buts.

We've stopped with a thump.
   I think we are stuck. That was no hole I could see, not even
                                              a slump.

We're halfway up the wheels in oozy mud
   And stones and mush and awful crud.

I'll get off and push. You can get on the hood
   And cheer me on. That will be good.

So The Horse got off and pushed as hard as he could,
   But the car wouldn't move. Are we stuck here for good?

Asked The Cow with a sigh.
  You've given pushing a good try.

We should call Triple A
  To hear what they say.

They'll be here in a while.
  We'll just sit here and smile.

And hope. There they are! They got here so quick.
  They'll know the right trick!

With a pull and then a shove.
  We're beginning to move!

Thanks and good bye. Now I can get back on the hood.
  The Cow answered, I'm back on the running board and tied
                                                        in good.

Oh, it is good to be home.
  When there's Mud Season, let's just not roam.

THE COW AND THE HORSE AND THE BIRTHDAY PLATE

The Horse sat on the running board, The Cow sat on the hood.
  I heard some music at the house on the hill. We could go look.
                                      Do you think we should?

Said The Cow to The Horse. Why not, said The Horse as he
                                        stood up tall.
  And The Cow slid off the hood and exclaimed, Oh look!
                                        I didn't fall.

So The Horse went off at a fast 'horse pace.'
  The Cow came along—she just could not race.

The house is lit up and the table is set.
  Here comes the family—a birthday, I'll bet.

Said The Horse to The Cow as he peered through the door.
  Let's go to the window where we can see more,

Said The Cow to The Horse as they circled the house.
  But we must be quiet, just like a mouse.

The Horse whispered softly, Look at that—a little boy's party!
  When a little girl piped up, I hope you're a smarty

And found the flower on the plate that is there just for you.
  It's special for birthdays and there's only one, not a few.

I found a tiny blue flower right there on the plate.
  Do you have one also? That would be great!

Oh no, said the girl, Not until my birthday when I'll get the plate.
　　I must put a check on the calendar to mark down my date.

I see a cake with candles all lit and burning.
　　There's a special plate for a birthday! That's what I'm learning.

That's right! agreed The Horse with The Cow.
　　We've learned so much. But it's time to be going back now.

Before it gets dark and we can't find our way.
　　And The Cow answered quietly, Oh yes. It's been such a
　　　　　　　　　　　　　　　　　　　　　　　　　wonderful day.

THE COW, THE HORSE AND THE TELEPHONE

The Cow sat on the running board, The Horse sat on the hood.
  I have a question you can answer, if you would.

Have you heard of a telephone? The Cow said loudly.
  I've heard they hang on a wall, The Horse said proudly.

But what is their use? The Cow inquired.
  I think they are for talking into. The Horse was inspired.

Why would you do that when all the cows are close by?
  Maybe some go away, The Horse tried to think. Why?

Well that seems like it's silly, The Cow was still worried.
  Maybe it's just humans. They may just be hurried

To get an answer or such.
  The Horse kept thinking, But what they need just can't be much.

So I guess that the phone won't last very long
  The Cow confidently said, On this I'm not wrong.

So The Cow and The Horse in their infinite wisdom
  Gave up on the 'phoning'—an excellent decision.

For what came next … and next … and next … and next …
  Can't even be written in a coherent text.

THE COW AND THE HORSE, THANKSGIVING

The Cow sat on the running board, The Horse sat on the hood.
  Thanksgiving is coming soon, The Cow remarked, At least
                                                                         it should.

Yes, said The Horse, I agree that's true,
  But I wonder how to celebrate, just what should we do?

We can have cranberries and sweet potatoes, but we can't
                                                               have turkey.
  He's our friend, The Cow decided.

You're right. We must not have turkey. I have an idea,
  The Horse confided.

If we can't have turkey, why don't we change our plan?
  We can go to Turkey—You know we can!

Said the Horse to the Cow, Tie your seat belt tight.
  And close your eyes for our flight.

I can feel us fly like the Magic Carpet of old,
  Said the Cow. We are truly bold.

Look, there is Turkey! The Horse exclaimed with delight.
  I can see from here on the hood. What an amazing sight!

Are those minarets I see? And a dome on a Mosque!
  The Cow sighed, What more could I ask?

This must be Constantinople. We are in Turkey! The Cow
                                                                 exclaimed.
  But it's not Constantinople, it's Istanbul, The Horse explained.

Istan Bull … The Cow mused, That's just great!
  Maybe this is where I'll find a mate!

But why did they change it? asked The Cow.
  Who knows, said The Horse. Only the Turks know now.

Look over there—there are rugs on the ground.
  Do they make them by hand? None seem to be round.

The Cow thought, I think it's time to go home.
  But this was surely a grand place to roam.

So check your seat belt tight, reminded The Horse.
  The Cow laughed and said, Of course, of course!

And so they closed their eyes tight and flew through the air
  Until they arrived back home with moments to spare.

What a wonderful trip! What a perfect Thanksgiving!
  The Cow added happily. And the turkey's still living!

And so the Cow and The Horse arrived home in one piece.
  Said the Horse to the Cow, Maybe next time, it's Greece!

THE COW AND THE HORSE, HELPING SANTA

The Cow sat on the running board, The Horse sat on the hood.
   Santa's busy working. He probably needs help. I bet we could,

Said The Horse to The Cow as he got off the hood, I really must
                        stretch, He added as he slid off and stood
   Ready to go, But I'm not in the mood

To go anywhere, As The Horse climbed back on the hood
   As you knew he would.

So now what shall we do? said the impatient Cow.
   Let's go see Santa—and I want to go now!

OK, said The Horse. Be sure to tighten the seat belt.
   I've done that already, The Cow said. What's that I felt?

We're flying now,
   Said The Horse to The Cow.

We're going straight up north to the Pole.
   We can help Santa's Elves. That can be our role.

I see the North Pole. It looks like a workshop,
   The Cow said to The Horse as their Magic Car came to a stop.

Let's go and find Santa, The Horse neighed with delight.
   The Cow added with glee, Just look at this sight!

And there I see Santa and Elves working too.
   Now we can ask just what we can do.

The Horse approached Santa, We'd like to help you.
   Good! replied Santa. Those presents—we have quite a few.

Those Elves are wrapping packages. They tie as they sing.
   You can put your hoof on the knot to hold down the string.

And so The Cow and The Horse had a wonderful time
   Helping Santa and his Elves. But back on the car we must climb.

I'm tired, said The Cow.
   We'll go back right now,

Said The Horse as he held the last knot.
   Thank you Santa. We had a great time. We liked it a lot,

Said the Cow and The Horse as they flew away.
   And Merry Christmas to all. Have a Great Day!

UNITED STATES

THE COW AND THE HORSE
GO TO NEW YORK

The Cow sat on the running board, The Horse sat on the hood.
                                  I'd like to go somewhere exciting.
  New York City sounds inviting,

Said The Horse to The Cow.
  Let's go right now!

Said The Cow in reply.
  You know we always fly.

So tie your seat belt tight.
  We must fly at a great height.

Said The Cow to The Horse.
  Of course, of course!

We must land between buildings that are very tall.
  The landing space may be quite small.

Said The Horse to The Cow, in a reassuring voice.
  He hoped he would make a good landing choice.

I can see far below and even the ocean!
  Isn't that water over there? Or is that just my notion?

Said The Cow to The Horse, as they flew quite high.
  Isn't that New York? We must not pass it by!

There's a large green space!
  I hope we land in that very place.

The Horse said to The Cow.
   Hold on! We're going to land right now!

It's Central Park and there's a horse pulling people!
   And I see a church with a very high steeple.

Said The Cow to The Horse.
   His answer, Of course, of course.

Untie your seatbelt, let's go for a trot.
   There is much to do. We'll see a lot!

Of buildings and cars and people. Oh my!
   Can we move in this traffic? Let's give it a try,

Said The Horse to The Cow.
   Do you think they'll allow

Us to trot on the street?
   Just look at all the traffic we'll meet!

We must be quick!
   People and cars and traffic lights are thick

If we want to see stuff.
   I'm getting a headache, said The Cow in a huff.

Let's take a rest, some grass would taste good.
   Maybe we should go back. I'll sit on the hood,

Said The Cow to The Horse.
　He gently replied, Of course, of course.

It's back to the green of Central Park.
　It may have been busy, but this trip was a lark!

Said The Horse to The Cow,
　We'll go back right now.

And so The Cow and The Horse landed safe and sound
　Back home in their car on their very own ground.

THE COW AND THE HORSE GO TO FLORIDA

The Cow sat on the running board. The Horse sat on the hood.
  Let's go to Florida. I'm really in the mood.

It's cold up here. There's so much snow.
  Let's just start the car, pack up and go,

Said The Cow to The Horse with a pleading voice.
  Of course, of course, if that's your choice.

Said The Horse with joy.
  We can swim in the ocean! Oh boy, oh boy!

That will be fun and it's warm there too.
  Tie your seat belt tight. We'll enjoy the view,

As we fly down there to the sandy beaches.
  Maybe a stop in Georgia to buy some peaches.

That sounds just perfect, agreed The Cow.
  I've tied my seat belt. Let's go right now.

I'm glad we are flying. We'll get to Florida fast.
  Was that Washington that we just passed?

I see the beautiful Capitol dome!
  Aren't you glad that this country's our home?

Is that Florida that is so long and thin?
  Asked The Cow with cheerful, hopeful grin.

We'll land right there on a sandy beach,
  Said The Horse, One that's very easy to reach.

The Cow untied her seat belt and climbed right out
   To feel the sand on her feet and just run about.

Have you put your feet in the water to get them wet?
   The Cow asked The Horse. Not yet, not yet.

Let's take that swim in the ocean right here.
   Then have a picnic. The car is quite near.

The Horse said to The Cow.
   Then we better head home. The sun's setting right now.

So they climbed back on their car and tied their seat belts tight
   And flew quickly home to get there before night.

We had a wonderful time, said The Cow. But too short.
   Should we take up swimming as our new kind of sport?

THE COW AND THE HORSE GO WEST

Let's go somewhere, said The Cow to The Horse.
   The Cow on the running board, The Horse on the hood,
                                              of course.

We could fly across the country and see the West,
   Said The Horse, I think that's best.

So they got out their map to plot their course.
   We can highlight it in yellow, offered The Horse.

Let's go to the ocean to see how it looks.
   I've seen lots of pictures, but only in books.

They show the waves crashing, or making a beautiful motion.
   I'm very excited to visit the ocean!

Said The Cow to The Horse. And I know there are surfboards
                                      that swimmers ride.
   They swim way out and come in on a wave or the tide.

That's surfing!? The Cow asked incredulously.
   Young people stand on a board most confidently

And look for a wave to ride on in
   To the beach—standing up? They all look so thin!

The Horse then reminded The Cow,
   If your seat belt is tied, we can go right now.

And so they took off over mountain and plain.
   And then over a range of mountains again.

What a wonderful country! The Cow added, Wow!
   The Horse then exclaimed, We can land right now!

Right there on the beach,
   Or on the long highway. It's easy to reach.

And I saw a big city, Los Angeles, I think.
   Said The Horse as he trotted to the Pacific to take a long drink.

But we've been to New York, said The Cow to The Horse.
   Let's go up the Coast. The highway will be our new course.

The Horse commented, We can trot right along watching out
                                              for the traffic.
   There are cars by the dozen and their speed is terrific.

Said The Cow to The Horse, This highway's a Freeway
   So we must be careful. They don't give us much leeway.

I forgot. We are here in the car.
   We aren't trotting along. We can go very far

Up the Coast in a just a short time.
   We can even try mountains. In our trusty car, they are easy
                                                        to climb.

But this road by the Coast is positively scary.
   On every mile of this road one must be wary.

Of course, and the ocean is often far down below.
   The Horse said confidently as he spoke to The Cow.

This Country is amazing! The Cow exclaimed to The Horse.
   I'm glad we came here and are taking this course.

It will be hard to go home—the views are so grand.
   I'm so glad we have come. We've seen much of our beautiful
                                                        land.

Yes, said The Horse. I'll turn the car around.
   We'll go back to the east. Again homeward bound.

It is now time to return to our home.
   But we've seen mountains and prairies and an ocean with
                                                         foam.

As they landed with care, right back in their spot
   The Horse sighed and exclaimed, That was fun. We must travel
                                                          a lot.

THE COW AND THE HORSE GO TO CHINATOWN

The Cow sat on the running board, The Horse sat on the hood.
   Have you ever visited Chinatown—We could go there for the
                                                      food?

Tie your seat belt tight.
   We'll fly over the mountains and plains and all through the night.

Look we're over Los Angeles. See the lights down below?
   We've landed in Chinatown! But look at the mountains with
                                                      snow!

We have no time to sightsee. I'm hungry just now.
   Look! That cafe seems to have Dim Sum. Let's try it somehow.

There are people at tables. Maybe we can use one.
   There are Chinese ladies with carts of food. We must try some.

Would you like some Sui Mai?
   That's pork in a biscuit. Let's give it a try.

Or Fun Cheong? That's shrimp steamed in a sheet made of rice.
   And Chinese broccoli and Chei Fang—rice soup—would be
                                                      nice.

For dessert, some egg custard. Then let's move along.
   It's off to the shops. That's where I belong,

Said The Cow with a smile.
   Of course, of course, replied The Horse. We've come many a
                                                                mile.

So many shops with all kinds of things.
   Dolls and Buddhas, red envelopes, folding fans and small
                                                           bells that ring.

Look in this window. There are fancy satin bags, both tiny and
                                                                    large.
   And chopsticks and more fans and statues. I wonder
                                            what they charge?

And there is a grocery with pots and pans and dishes too.
   They are so pretty—mostly white and Chinese blue.

I like those small crockery pots filled with food that's preserved.
   The pots could be vases. We could enjoy their beauty, which
                                                          they deserve.

What a wonderful place—a feast for the eyes.
   And so much for so little. A real taste of China in a small size.

But we better head home. We have loaded the car.
   Tie your seat belt again. We must travel quite far.

Good. Now we are back from a wonderful trip.
   Where we tasted another country without going by ship.

THE COW AND THE HORSE TRAVEL TO MINNESOTA

The Cow sat on the running board, The Horse sat on the hood.
   We should see Minnesota—we really should.

The Cow said to The Horse.
   Of course, of course.

That's true. You are exactly right.
   Tighten your seat belt. Are you all set for the flight?

Look at that long ribbon of road
   With toy cars and trucks. Some trucks have a tiny enormous
                                                          load.

But we must fly on. There's a lake to our right.
   We'll see the skyscrapers of Chicago before it is night.

Then it's over Illinois and Wisconsin's trees and farms
   And west to Minnesota with all of its charms.

Across the St. Croix. We're here at last.
   I must admit, this trip's been a blast!

Said The Horse with an excited Neigh!
   I'm so glad we have come this way.

Added The Cow.
   But do you think we could land just now?

Minneapolis is beautiful with lakes right in town
   Where people walk and people run and people swim and even
                                                           lie down

To rest or enjoy a peaceful sail or swim
   Or a run around the lake. Here at Calhoun, life just can't be grim.

Said The Horse to The Cow.
   This is a chance for a little rest now.

Did you notice the names, Hiawatha, Nokomis and Minnehaha too?
   The Ojibwes lived here and left their names, quite a few.

Explorers, Nicollet and Hennepin, and fur traders came here.
   There are pine trees and oak trees and in the woods lots of deer.

But let's go on up north. It is easy driving up there.
   The horizon's far off. There is just land and fresh air.

This road is a ribbon just as straight as can be!
   The land is as flat as a pancake. Look at all the farms we can see!

Said The Cow to The Horse.
   He replied, It's amazing, of course, of course.

Look! We've reached the Canadian border.
   We'll have lunch by the Lake. Please place an order

For walleyed pike caught fresh from the Lake.
   A lunch like this is not hard to take.

It's time, I think we better head home. This trip has been fun.
   But, first look down there. That's where iron used to be mined
                                                              by the ton!

Oh my goodness! We missed the Capital, St Paul.
   That is too bad, I'm truly sorry, but I guess we can't see it all.

I see our own pasture. It's good to be home.
   To see more of our country, we must continue to roam.

THE COW AND THE HORSE AND SHEBOYGAN

The Cow sat on the running board, The Horse sat on the hood.
  I'd like to go to Sheboygan. I'm hoping that we could,

Said The Cow, and so replied The Horse,
  Of course, of course.

But what is Sheboygan, and where?
  It's a city in Wisconsin. We'll find the way there.

So they fastened their seat belts and were on their way
  Over Chicago—they'll get there today.

There is Sheboygan with a sandy Lake Michigan beach.
  We can land there. It's not hard to reach.

Look to your left up that slight hill.
  It's an older mansion, I think—and well kept still.

Let's look in the window. There's a party perhaps.
  A table with guests seated. Linen napkins in their laps!

That bouquet is gorgeous with flowers galore.
  I think it's a birthday, a family gathering. There's no room for
                                            more.

It looks like there is space for each person to sleep.
  And plenty of time for talk and walk, but complaints, not a
                                            peep.

Let's go around the house and peek in the windows.
  This mansion is huge—it just grows and grows.

There is a note inside the front door!
   'Happy 90th birthday!' It says, 'And we hope many more!'

I was right. It is a birthday and the mansion is grand.
   With the family all here, this event was well planned.

But let's look at Sheboygan. No Walmart in sight.
   Just small single stores with treasures, a delight.

The scenery is lovely along this back road.
   It leads to a small town that is charming, I'm told.

We could explore Wisconsin—it's famous for cheese.
   But let's go back to the party again, if you please.

To see such a gathering is beautiful and rare.
   Now let's return home in our car that we share.

The Horse looked at The Cow, and wrinkled his brow,
   We do travel to great places. I'm not sure just how.

FOREIGN TRAVEL

THE COW AND THE HORSE GO TO NORWAY

The Cow sat on the running board, The Horse sat on the hood.
   How would you like to go to Norway? I think we should.

Said The Horse to The Cow. We could go up the coast
   The midnight sun's out all day. We could see the most

Of everything. Tie your seat belt tight. We're on our way.
   Look over there. I think that's a bay—

It must be Bergen where we catch the boat
   That carries the mail and passengers, and has stayed afloat

In good weather and bad—to the Arctic Circle and back.
   The Captain knows the way. He always keeps track.

I can feel the boat moving past that busy dock.
   There are high mountains and inlets—and we can see 'round
                                       the clock!'

We'll stay on the deck. We wouldn't fit in a cabin and we'd be
                                                             inside.
   Oh look at the mountains and fjords and a village we're
                                                     stopping beside.

The houses are painted all colors and hues.
   There go the people, the mail and all of the news.

But it's on up the coast. We're going farther up north.
   This craft is steady. We don't rock back and forth.

The mountains are huge. I hear that Trolls live up there.
   They are enormous and ugly, have tails and long hair!

They say that they're dumb, but very scary too
   So if we see one, what should we do?

Run like the dickens. I hear they are slow.
   But don't look back, because their shadow will grow.

Troll Fjorden is next. It's a special spot on our way.
   If the weather is right we can go in, but not stay.

We'll leave Troll Fjorden so the Trolls can live there.
   There are no houses for humans—we just wouldn't dare,

Said the Captain as he maneuvered the ship.
   It takes up the whole fjord—he can't make a slip

In the turn of the wheel. Oh good we made it all right
   Now it's on to Trondheim. Everyone can alight.

There is the Nidaros Cathedral built in eleven hundred or so
   With statues on the back wall of disciples we know.

Or maybe we don't. They just stand there with dubious
                                       expressions.
   They may have had too many of St. Olaf's stern sessions.

Look at the racks of fish hanging to dry!
   In the endless sun and the brilliant blue sky.

We're moving again—The Arctic Circle is next.
   Oh look! There are LappLanders, even reindeer to add to this
                                                                text.

But we're at the top of the world—it's time to go home
   There's so much to see. We'll later add to this tome.

THE COW AND THE HORSE
GO TO NORWAY AGAIN

The Cow sat on the running board, The Horse sat on the hood.
   Let's go back to Norway and even try their food.

Ok. Tie your seat belt tight and we're on our way.
   In the cities and country is where we'll stay.

We'll land in Oslo and stay right there
   Till we've seen the Kon-Tiki and the Viking ship and wonders
                                                 to spare.

There's a Museum with a farmhouse we can go in and look
   To see how they once lived and how they cooked

With old iron stoves or over a fire
   That heats the room too! Oh how they must tire

Of cooking and cleaning and making their clothes
   And weaving the cloth and knitting their hose,

Said The Cow to The Horse.
   And The Horse answered, Of course, of course.

There's a Stave Church made of very old pine.
   It was built during the Middle Ages. Such a unique design.

But let's go to Flekkefjord along the south coast,
   Where our friend's Grand Dad was born and they eat cheese
                                                called Gjetost.

The small farm is at the end of a lane.
   To get there we'll pass houses and farms and the fjord now
                                                and again.

The house has been here a very long time
   Midst trees and water and that big hill to climb.

But we must go to Bergen to see the Grieg home, Troldhaugen
   And the Fish Market and Hanseatic buildings along the water
                                                  again.

We didn't know this when we went up the coast
   But the buildings are World Famous—of these Norway can
                                                  boast.

Do you like the food, Lutefisk, Lefse and Cod?
   If you're not Norwegian, these are certainly odd.

Now it's time to go home and dream of our travels
   And write this all down before it unravels.

THE COW AND THE HORSE
GO TO SCOTLAND

The Cow sat on the running board, The Horse sat on the hood.
   Let's go to Scotland. I really think we should,

Said The Cow to The Horse.
   A great idea! said The Horse. Of course, of course!

Is your seat belt tight?
   We're off on our flight

Over the ocean. Look we're landing in Scotland!
   There's a big house! A Manor House at hand.

We can headquarter there and look around.
   This house is huge, rooms and rooms to be found.

The Cow spoke up, Let's go into Edinburgh. There's a castle
                                                    to see.
   We haven't visited an ancient castle. What history there'll be!

Oh look, there's a palace at the end of this long hill.
   It's Holyrood Palace. Every year Queen Elizabeth stays here still.

It has been here since before the 16th Century.
   The stories abound with myth and mystery.

What an interesting place, but let's see the Military Tattoo. It's on
                                                    tonight
   At the Castle. Bands from the whole world! We can't miss that
                                                        sight.

Then let's go to South Queensferry on the Firth of Forth. It's near by.
   We can take the train, or at least we can try.

Do you think there's a cattle car, or can we have a seat?
   A ride in a coach would be really neat.

Robert Louise Stevenson stayed at an Inn in South Queensferry.
   Before there was a bridge the Queen took a boat. But the
                                        sailors were wary.

So a bridge was built to carry the traffic.
   And everyone thought that that was terrific.

We must visit a Scottish Tartan textile mill,
   To see the colors, the perfect weaving would be a thrill!

Said The Cow to The Horse. And The Horse replied,
   We couldn't do that if we tried and tried.

And The Cow added, wearily, For now, let's go home.
   We can always come back. There is much more of Scotland
                                             to roam.

THE COW AND THE HORSE VISIT ENGLAND

The Horse sat on the running board, The Cow sat on the hood.
  We're on our way to London. This trip sounds very good!

Look down there! There's London Bridge and the Tower close by.
  We can land by the Bridge and see the Tower too, if we try.

The Cow was excited, See the Beefeaters in their traditional uniforms.
  They've guarded the Tower for centuries in sun, snow and storms.

The Crown Jewels are well guarded, but Anne Boleyn isn't there now.
  Let's go to Buckingham Palace to see the changing of the guard, said The Horse to The Cow.

There are the theaters and shops and museums too.
  There's too much to see. There's just too much to do.

We must remember that London was bombed, skeleton buildings everywhere.
  St. Paul's Cathedral was saved. That, they could never spare.

Now London's back to normal, the people cheerful and busy.
  The splendor of Buckingham Palace made me quite dizzy.

Let's go on to Windsor. I hear the country is fine.
  And we can see Windsor Castle. It's older than time—

Oh! It is beautiful with the Round Tower there on the hill
   And the swans in the river. The whole scene gives me a thrill,

Said The Cow as she gazed at the Palace and then went inside.
   It is all so amazing. The Doll House for Queen Mary has
                                        nothing to hide.

There is a wine cellar with wine, a library with books you can read.
   And a Hoover vacuum cleaner, anything a child or a Princess
                                        could need.

We should follow the Thames and we could see the Colleges at
                                        Oxford.
   And then on to Stratford-upon-Avon and a Shakespeare play
                                        we could afford.

Though the English countryside is charming
   With beautiful cottages, flower gardens and small farming,

There is so much to see and so much to learn.
   We are thrilled each time we take a turn.

It's too much to take in. Let's go home soon.
   We can always come back—It's not as far as the moon!

And so they got home before the sun set
   With fond memories of England, some of the very best yet.

THE COW AND THE HORSE GO TO PARIS

The Cow sat on the running board, The Horse sat on the hood.
　Have you ever been to Paris? Let's just go. Do you think we
　　　　　　　　　　　　　　　　　　　　　　　　could?

Said The Cow to The Horse with her hopes up high.
　Tie your seatbelt tight. We'll give it a try, said The Horse with a
　　　　　　　　　　　　　　　　determined gleam in his eye.

We'll fly through the night and land at De Gaulle.
　Oh no! That's too far out. That's no good at all!

Said The Cow. Let's land at the Seine.
　We can look at the bookstalls, and then look again.

Of course, said The Horse, We'll be right in the middle.
　We can look at The Arch and we won't have to fiddle

Around with a map
　At least not right away, 'cuz we'll need a nap.

To get ready to see all the places there are.
　From the Arch, the Eiffel Tower's not very far.

And then back to the Seine and the Ile de la Cité.
　There are Notre-Dame and Sainte-Chapelle, the stained glass
　　　　　　　　　　　　　　　　windows are worth a long stay.

Then it's on to the Left Bank. The Sorbonne is there.
　And the Luxembourg Gardens. It just isn't fair—

There's too much to see and window shop too.
   In Cartier's windows those are real diamonds. It's true!

And when we are there Place de la Concorde and the old Opéra
                                                          are near
   And Sacre-Coeur is in sight. The steps are many, but we can
                                                          climb, never fear.

Down the other side is the Flea Market so full
   Of stuff of all kinds. We could be there until

We need some coffee. We'll go back to Des Champs Elysées
   And sit outside at a Café to watch the crowds pass our way.

Maybe they'll buy some flowers to take home, just for fun,
   Or stop at a pâtisserie for a baguette and a bun.

It's fun to sit here and watch the people walk by.
   Just to rest awhile, enjoy the coffee and sigh—

We must come back for The Louvre and Montmartre. There's no
                                     'best' to Paris; it's all fascinating.
   We must come back. No procrastinating.

But now let's go home. It's just too much to take.
   We can sleep when we get there and remember when we're
                                                                 awake.

THE COW AND THE HORSE
GO TO BORDEAUX

The Cow sat on the running board, The Horse sat on the hood.
   Let's go to Bordeaux, France. I've always wished we could,

Said The Cow. Bordeaux has been there ever since it was Gaul.
   I've even heard there's still part of the Roman Wall.

That sounds great. Tie your seat belt tight.
   We'll be there in the morning if we travel all night.

We've crossed the ocean and are safely down.
   Let's look around before we go into town.

There's a small road. Let's follow that
   Through villages and vineyards. The land is quite flat.

The villages are quaint and quiet—no billboard to read—
   Just open doors to invite one in to get what we need.

That is hard to do when we are used to pictures of stuff
   To pick from and point to and tell us when we have enough.

But let's move along. Let's try that small lane.
   It goes through a cornfield. Look what we've gained!

A beautiful monument with a tall column too,
   Dedicated to six Resistance fighters who lost their lives, but to
                                      France they were true.

What a wonderful find—a memorial lost in a field.
   To the Resistance in Vichy who just did not yield.

It's on to Bordeaux. Let's not go slow.
   We're in the center of town and ready to go!

There's the St. Andrew's Cathedral. It surely stands out.
   Where Eleanor of Aquitaine married the Crown Prince of France
                     in the eleven hundreds, or there about.

There is a bookstore with English books too.
   What a good store to have—if we stayed we'd have reading
                                          to do.

And buses go by going out to the suburbs
   Where it's quiet and no one disturbs

A person all day so those books can be read.
   On the weekends, adventure! Exploring back roads instead.

But that's if we lived here, The Horse then replied.
   We just must come back! The Cow hopefully cried.

Now it's time to head home,
   To gather some energy for the next place we roam.

THE HORSE AND THE COW VISIT BORDEAUX II

The Cow sat on the running board, The Horse sat on the hood.
   We visited Paris, let's visit Bordeaux. Don't you think we
                                                  really should?

Yes, let's do. We'll see the South of France
   The weather's great. It's our perfect chance

To see the vineyards and city too.
   There'll be a lot to do.

So tie your seat belt and hang on tight.
   We're over the ocean—we'll fly through the night.

I see the lights of Bordeaux down below.
   We're landing in the center of town. We're ready to go!

Look at that fountain with huge bronze horses on each side
                                                  looking at us.
   What are you doing there? You must have a lot to discuss.

We do, answered a Mythical Horse.
   We're called Gerondic Horses, in their honor, of course.

And then during World War II we were stolen to melt us down
   To make ammunition of us, said the Bronze Horse with a frown.

But some men of the French Resistance rescued us and hid us.
   They were then shot and we were lost when the War ended—
                                                  such a fuss.

Many years later we were found in a wine cave
    And brought back to our places. Those men were so brave.

Thanks for asking, our history is rare.
    It's nice to know that you really care.

Thank you! said The Horse. Your story is fascinating.
    But it's back to the coast—the ocean is invigorating.

Let's go along the coast to Biarritz.
    It's a beautiful vacation spot where everyone fits,

Except for the Jews during World War II.
    This sign says 400 picked up, not just a few.

The Cow noticed the bank of hydrangea: pink, red and blue.
    I've never seen so many colors! There are quite a few!

This trip has been fun and we've learned quite a bit.
    There's much to remember. I must write it down before I forget.

But I'm tired. And I want to go home, said The Cow.
    So let's go back and rest for now.

The Horse answered, Of course, of course. We'll head home
    And come back again to just roam and roam.

THE COW AND THE HORSE
TRAVEL THE MIDI CANAL

The Cow sat on the running board. The Horse sat on the hood.
   Have you heard of The Midi Canal? It's in France and very old.
                             We should see it, we really should.

But what's a canal? Tell me if you can,
   Said The Cow. It is like a river, but it is built by man,

Replied The Horse who knew a lot about many things.
   Like places to go and things to see and even cabbages and
                                           kings.

Let's fly there and find it and then rent a barge.
   They'll teach us to drive it, and then we're in charge.

Tie your seatbelt tight. We are starting right now.
   We're off to Southeast France! We'll find it somehow.

Toulouse is where we rent the barge and take stock.
   We'll learn to drive straight ahead and stop at each lock.

We'll stop at each lock until it becomes the right height
   And then dock at the canal edge to sleep for the night.

We're here and moving along as we should
   Past lines of trees and a path. By foot or bike would also be
                                           good.

That village has a Festival. Let's stop and attend.
   There's music and dancing, but we can't stay until the end—

We must stop for the night and then move along
    To Carcassonne, the walled city that's been there so long.

This canal is three hundred years old and always in use.
    It is beautiful and clean. It's had care, not abuse.

To stay used and helpful and a treat for the eyes
    To the history of France it must have many ties.

This slow moving barge and old tall leafy trees
    The path along the water and sometimes a breeze.

But the quiet along so many interesting scenes.
    It would be hard to find on a movie screen.

The locks are a challenge, and to feel the boat rise—
    Water poured in, or water drained out, which one is wise.

A wonderful experience with a new countryside
    But it's time to go home and relive this boat ride.

THE COW AND THE HORSE
GO TO HONG KONG

The Cow sat on the running board, The Horse sat on the hood.
  Do you know where Hong Kong is? Yes? I knew you would.

Said The Cow to The Horse. Do you think we can go?
  Of course, of course, but we can't be slow.

We'll go there right now.
  Tie you seat belt tight. I know you know how.

Look down! Look down! It looks like toy blocks standing on end!
  I'm leaning over to look till my back just can't bend

Anymore. Are we going to land? Is there any room down there?
  You are a very good driver. You take such great care

In landing our car.
  Everything is close. Nothing is far!

Said The Cow to The Horse.
  Of course, of course.

Come, get out and let's walk. Just look around and see what you like.
  We'll look in Kowloon. It's not a great hike.

And then Hong Kong Island before coming back for a bite
  Of lunch of Dim Sum. That is just right.

There are as many people as buildings—mostly Chinese, but others too.
  I wonder what all of these people do?

Do you like Dim Sum? There are many small dishes.
   It's fun to try them. Most are very delicious.

There are shops galore on these crowded streets
   With fascinating artwork and Chinese treats.

These buildings are so tall you can't see the sky
   Only a patch of blue or a small cloud passing by.

But look down at the Harbor! It has ships galore!
   From ancient junks to the QE II and just maybe a million more.

This is all much too much. My head's starting to ache.
   Let's find our car and head back to our state

Of calm and wide spaces that we call home.
   But I wouldn't miss Hong Kong. We must continue to roam.

THE COW AND THE HORSE GO TO SINGAPORE

The Cow sat on the running board, The Horse sat on the hood.
   The Horse spoke up, How about going really far. I'm in a 'far
                                                             off' mood.

And let's do something new. Do you know Singapore?
   At Christmas it couldn't be a bore.

Said The Cow with high hopes,
   Good Idea. Get ready, tie that rope

That's your seat belt very tight.
   We'll be over the ocean through most of the night.

I see colored lights on buildings below.
   Could it be Singapore? I'd like to know,

Said The Cow as The Horse landed the car.
   It's Singapore! We've come very far,

Said The Horse. Those lights are huge decorations
   Of Santa and Christmas and much celebration!

Singapore is very clean. No trash or chewing gum allowed.
   Not even in a noisy crowd.

The Raffles Hotel where Somerset Maugham wrote is nearby.
   Let's rest and have Tea and give it a try.

That was fun, even peanuts on the floor by the Bar.
   But let's do some shopping, that can't be too far.

There is a parade of people and an Elephant too,
    All pictured on cloth. That's certainly new

To me, but that is Batik as old as can be.
    And there's cloth for a Sari, I'd like to see.

Now where would you like to go? said The Cow to The Horse.
    Let's go to the Park where animals live. Of course!

Said the Cow. Then we must go home.
    It's such fun to travel and to stop and to roam.

But home would be nice and comfortable.
    And then we could travel again as long as we're able.

So The Cow and The Horse flew back in their car.
    Since no place on the globe is ever too far.

THE COW AND THE HORSE
GO TO THAILAND

The Cow sat on the running board, The Horse sat on the hood.
   The Horse spoke up, Let's go to Bangkok, I'm really in the
                                                    mood.

The Cow was puzzled. What's in Bangkok, and where is it?
   It's the capital of Thailand and they have Queen Sirikit.

She did many kind things for the country she loves.
   Teaching art and crafts and weaving and maybe even making
                                                    gloves.

She's helped in all kinds of ways.
   She's been honored all over the world for the help she's
                                                    displayed.

Tie your seatbelt tight, we're on our way
   To Thailand! This will be a great day!

The Cow was excited. Look, we're landing beside a small pond!
   There are huge turtles and shrubs trimmed like elephants and
                                          a small palace beyond.

This is amazing, but the Craft Village is ahead.
   There are hand-forged tools and woodwork about which you
                                                    have read.

Said The Cow to The Horse as they scampered along
   Right up to the Weaver's Room—large and oblong.

Look at the very fine fabric she makes!
   It takes skill and good eyesight. There are no mistakes.

Or they are raveled back and brought to perfection.
   The Weaver's proud of her work—the fabric resembles a
                                                  confection.

In Bangkok there's a Silk Store, Jim Thompson started it
   So the Thais could sell their fabric and the World could then
                                                  profit.

But we must go home. What a beautiful day.
   Such an interesting visit, I could just stay and stay.

Said The Cow to The Horse as they got back in their car.
   We'll be home before dark. Home is never too far.

THE COW AND THE HORSE GO TO BALI

The Horse sat on the running board. The Cow sat on the hood.
  Have you heard of Bali? I've heard the food is good.

Tie your seat belt tight and we're on our way.
  It's in the exotic South Seas. We'll have a special holiday!

There it is! Just where it is supposed to be!
  We'll land right now and see what we can see.

We'll park right here on the beach.
  And splurge on a hotel that's easy to reach

From all the places we'll go.
  But where are all the places? I think a guide would know.

Oh yes. I'll take you to a village up in the hills.
  On the way we'll stop for an elephant ride just for the thrills.

Look there's a school out for lunch.
  Their dishes are leaves from a banana bunch!

The Cow cried, The Guide's driving on the edge of the hill on a two-rut path!
  Don't look out this window! We could go over the edge and crash!

Notice the small houses of wood, The Guide said. It's a family compound.
  There is a house for eating and a house for sleeping and even one where the deceased can be found.

Cremation of bodies is an elaborate celebration.
   It's a time to release the Soul from the body of their relation.

Look! The Cow said, There's a line of beautiful women on their way to the temple,
   Carrying towers of flowers and food on their heads. It looks so simple!

Their posture is perfect, their walk slow and in line.
   An unreal vision. It is truly sublime,

Marveled The Cow, But let's go on to the city where carving wood is a skill.
   To see such talent is yet another thrill.

And fabric, handwoven in Ikat design
   We've seen talents and beauty beyond reason or rhyme.

Look! There are small plates of flowers placed on the street!
   And statues of small gods, but clothed—all very neat.

There's a special dinner at the hotel.
   Fresh fruit and barbecue. I think I can smell

It from here. But it's starting to rain! A real monsoon!
   We're soaked to the skin! We'll just slip and slide to our room!

We've seen so much, my mind's all a flutter.
   Let's just go home and sort out our mind's clutter.

Yes. Tie your seat belt tight. We can take a straight course.
   And we'll be right back home, wearily sighed The Horse.

THE COW AND THE HORSE GO TO SIBERIA

The Horse sat on the running board, The Cow sat on the Hood.
   Do you know about Siberia? I've heard it's a place not well
                                                           understood.

Let's go and find out.
   We'll fly over China. That's an interesting route.

There's the Forbidden City in the center of Beijing!
   What amazing sights this adventure might bring.

We're already on the Russo-Chinese border.
   Look at those trains, they are changing their wheels! That's an
                                                                                     order.

Because the track widths, or gauges are different,
   And I guess they are permanent.

We'll go on to Chita, a large city six time zones away
   From the capital, Moscow. It does, or doesn't hold sway.

Look! We're here! There are buildings galore.
   And apartments and beautiful old wooden houses. We couldn't
                                                                           ask for more.

Let's land and take a walk around.
   There are two or three colleges and more sights to be found.

There's a large patch of green, the City Square
   With a huge library and a blue church. Let's land. There is room
                                                                               to spare.

And a statue of Lenin, but Stalin's not there.
    What a history has Russia, but not often fair.

The Decembrists arrived in 1825.
    They had challenged the Czar. To Siberia! he said. And walk,
                                                      don't drive!

And then their wives came too and started schools
    And the library. Their wits and their wisdom were valuable tools.

The apartment houses are flimsy, but the Veterans Hospital is fine.
    The Veterans are heroes. They stood by their line

At Leningrad for almost three years.
    These Veterans, survivors have smiles, not tears.

This visit has been great, but it leaves much to be done.
    We must visit the schools and Steppes. Our visit has hardly
                                                              begun.

For now, let's go home but return to see more.
    It's hard to imagine what more is in store.

THE COW AND THE HORSE
GO BACK TO SIBERIA

The Cow sat on the running board, The Horse sat on the hood.
  We must go back to Siberia. You know we promised we would,

Said The Cow being hopeful, to the Horse.
  His enthusiastic answer was, Of course, of course.

So their seat belts were tied tight in a second.
  And they arrived in Chita even sooner than they had reckoned.

Let's look in these windows. It looks like a school
  For young girls learning their 3 R's but also sewing, crocheting
                and even bobbin lace! That's really cool!

And another class is doing Russian dancing and special Russian
                                  singing.
  The old traditions are still taught along with the added
                                  technology.
  They seem to cover everything.

And look in this building there's a party for guests.
  The food is served on Khokhloma, decorated wooden dishes.
  The dishes must be their best.

Let's go out in the country, I think it's called the Steppes, and find
                                  a village or such.
  The road is a dirt road not traveled much.

The Cow spoke up, Nothing seems modern. The villages are old
                                                                           and small.
    I wonder where they shop. We haven't seen even one mall.

Look, there's a pillar and people in costumes standing there.
    They are welcoming someone. We can stand aside and just
                                                                                                 stare.

These are Buryat people who came long ago.
    They are welcoming friends with blue scarves and tea in a bowl.

We'll follow along; they are going to a school
    That has an American teacher. The kids read a Thank You,
                                smiled broadly and follow the rule.

Now the grown-ups are going to a new building to a special
                                                                        luncheon for all.
    Look! They're giving toasts and speeches and special songs!
                                                    They are having a ball!

The whole group is going to the sacred Mount Alkhanai, now a
                                                                       National Park.
    The Dalai Lama visited and enjoyed it. It is now a famous
                                                                       landmark.

Said The Cow to The Horse,
    Who agreed, You are right, of course, of course.

There is a new Buddhist Temple with student monks chanting
 their prayers.
 This is a wonderful place. Everyone is friendly; no one puts
 on 'airs'.

So it is back through the Steppes over the dirt road,
 Past villages and farms and old cars with people, their load.

Villagers and farmers going home at the end of the day.
 A lonely, strange place. Would we want to stay?

Let's stop in Chita to say goodbye to our friends.
 With sad waves, but great thanks to Siberia this journey ends.

It's good to be home and rest for awhile
 Before we take off on many a new mile.

Rate this book on our website!

www.novumpublishing.com

The author

Jean Dickinson grew up in Northern Minnesota, but has had the opportunity to call many places home. She loves reading, writing, knitting, and especially travel. She met her husband when the GIs came home after WWII and together they lived on the GI Bill. Their combined love of adventure motivated them to spend their savings on biking in Europe one summer soon after WWII. Since Jean did not want a professional career, she has been free to live and raise children in 15 different localities. This lifestyle gave her the opportunity to travel extensively. The Cow and The Horse arrived one night, and they have provided her with the opportunity to retrace many of her adventures. This is not the end of her travels, or those for The Cow and The Horse!

novum 🔖 PUBLISHER FOR NEW AUTHORS

The publisher

> *He who stops getting better stops being good.*

This is the motto of novum publishing, and our focus is on finding new manuscripts, publishing them and offering long-term support to the authors.
Our publishing house was founded in 1997, and since then it has become THE expert for new authors and has won numerous awards.

Our editorial team will peruse each manuscript within a few weeks free of charge and without obligation.

You will find more information about
novum publishing and our books on the internet:

www.novumpublishing.com

www.ingramcontent.com/pod-product-compliance
Lightning Source LLC
LaVergne TN
LVHW041634070426
835507LV00008B/612